Who Was
Langston Hughes?

by Billy Merrell

illustrated by Gregory Copeland

Penguin Workshop

For Dana Thomas, my seventh-grade English
teacher, and the first to call me a writer—BM

PENGUIN WORKSHOP
An imprint of Penguin Random House LLC, New York

First published in the United States of America by Penguin Workshop,
an imprint of Penguin Random House LLC, New York, 2024

Visit us online at penguinrandomhouse.com.

Library of Congress Cataloging-in-Publication Data is available.

Printed in the United States of America

ISBN 9780593658543 (paperback)   10 9 8 7 6 5 4 3 2 1 WOR
ISBN 9780593658550 (library binding)   10 9 8 7 6 5 4 3 2 1 WOR

Contents

Who Was Langston Hughes?

In 1925, twenty-three-year-old Langston Hughes was working as a busboy, clearing tables at the Wardman Park Hotel in Washington, DC. One day, he read in the newspaper that a very famous poet named Vachel Lindsay was in town.

Mr. Lindsay, a white man from Illinois, was scheduled to read his poems at the same hotel where Langston worked.

Langston had seen many famous people at the hotel. Important politicians and diplomats stayed there all the time. But they didn't excite Langston. The idea of meeting a famous poet did.

Langston, who wrote poetry every chance he could, desperately wanted to attend the poetry reading. But he knew the hotel didn't allow Black people into the auditorium.

That day, during his shift, Langston saw the poet eating in the dining room. He recognized him from the picture in the newspaper. Langston knew that he could lose his job if he tried to talk to Mr. Lindsay while he was eating, but he had to do something!

Langston wrote out three of his own poems and put them in his pocket. When no one was watching, he walked up to Mr. Lindsay. He didn't know what to say to such a famous poet. So he simply told the man how much he admired his poems. Then Langston reached into his pocket and quietly put his poems on the table. Then he hurried back to the kitchen.

Later, while Langston was clearing a table, he saw Mr. Lindsay reading the poems he had handed him!

What Langston didn't know was that Mr. Lindsay later read those poems aloud to the large audience who had come to hear him speak. No one expected Vachel Lindsay to read poems by someone else. Especially not poems by a Black man who worked at the hotel! But the people in the audience liked Langston's poems.

The next morning, on his way to work, Langston read the newspaper again. This time, there was an article about *him*! The piece explained that Mr. Lindsay had discovered a "Negro busboy poet." (*Negro* was a word used to describe Black people at the time. Today, it is considered offensive.)

When Langston arrived at work, there were reporters waiting. They interviewed him and took his picture. They asked him to pose wearing his white uniform and hat, holding up a tray of dirty dishes in the middle of the dining room.

Langston didn't want to tell the reporters they were wrong. In a sense, Vachel Lindsay *had* discovered him. It wasn't often that he had *white* readers. But in Harlem, a mostly Black neighborhood in New York City, Langston had already been discovered. In fact, he was very well-known there to a huge Black audience, and his first book was about to come out from a major publisher.

The story about Langston Hughes was soon reprinted in newspapers from Maine to Florida. No one had ever heard of a "Negro busboy poet," and everyone wanted to see what Langston looked like. Langston was happy to have the publicity.

Back at the hotel, there was a package waiting for Langston. It contained books that Mr. Lindsay had left for him. The poet had also written Langston a long note, full of helpful advice. Langston followed that advice and quit his job at the Wardman Park Hotel. It wasn't long before people all over the country—and the world—knew about Langston Hughes.

Langston went on to be the most famous African American poet there has ever been. In fact, he's among the most famous American poets of all time. More famous than even Vachel Lindsay.

CHAPTER 1
Growing Up Black

James Mercer Langston Hughes was born in Joplin, Missouri, on February 1, 1902.

Langston's father had studied law. But he was not a lawyer when Langston was born. Black people in Missouri were not allowed to be lawyers at that time. Even if Mr. Hughes moved Langston's family to a state with fairer laws, it would not have helped. White clients would not hire Black lawyers. And few Black clients could afford a lawyer at all.

Langston's father had little hope that things would improve for his family. Mr. Hughes wanted to leave the United States. In Mexico, he could practice law. Langston's mother didn't speak Spanish, so she could not work there. But she agreed to learn. And they decided to move. But Mexico was not what they expected. When they arrived in Mexico City, in April of 1907, there was an earthquake! Sidewalks and streets cracked open. Tarantulas and scorpions climbed out of the walls! Langston's mother was not happy. She immediately decided to return with Langston to the United States. Mr. Hughes stayed. Langston's mother got a job in Topeka, Kansas. But the job didn't pay enough for her to take care of Langston. She wanted her son to have a happy childhood. She sent him to live with his grandmother, Mary Langston, in Lawrence, Kansas—at least until she could find a better job.

Mary Langston

Mary, whose family name young Langston had been given, was one of the first women to attend Oberlin College in Ohio. She had been married to two abolitionists, people who fought to end slavery. Her second husband, Langston's grandfather, was a political activist. He was the brother of John Mercer Langston, the first African American from Virginia elected to the United States Congress.

John Mercer Langston

Mary Langston told her grandson stories about all these men, along with other Black leaders and freedom fighters.

Mary Langston was a proud woman. Her grandmother was Cherokee and her grandfather was a French tradesman. And though Mary was

Black, none of her ancestors had been enslaved. So she refused to do work once reserved for enslaved people. She never washed strangers' clothes or cleaned other people's houses. Instead she made money by renting rooms in her house.

Mary and Langston lived modestly. They ate salt pork and wild dandelion greens. For entertainment, Mary would sit in her rocker and talk to her grandson. She read to him from the Bible and told him long stories from memory.

Washington and Du Bois

At the turn of the twentieth century, Booker T. Washington and W. E. B. Du Bois were the two leading Black social reformers. They had very different ideas of how to solve problems of race in the United States following the Civil War.

Washington had been born into slavery in Virginia and believed Black people should try to fit into the communities where they lived. He stressed education, with an emphasis on practical job skills. Washington told his followers that financial stability came from working hard and would earn them the respect of their white neighbors.

Booker T. Washington

Du Bois was born free in Massachusetts and believed Black people should move to areas of the country that were more accepting. He stressed education, with an emphasis on writing and other forms of expression.

Du Bois told his followers that by creating and celebrating a uniquely African American culture, Black people would earn the respect of white Americans.

W. E. B. Du Bois

She also taught young Langston about history.
She told him about the town of Lawrence, where
they lived. It had been founded by abolitionists,
both Black and white. Lawrence had once been

a meeting place for people who didn't believe in slavery. Everyone was allowed to enter the churches, hotels, restaurants, and other businesses, regardless of their race.

Lawrence, Kansas, 1898

By the time Langston moved to Lawrence in 1908, though, the town had changed. It had become segregated, with strict rules about where Black people were allowed to go.

White boys Langston's age could swim at the YMCA or join the Boy Scouts. They could take part in school track meets and watch Charlie Chaplin movies at the theater. Langston could do none of these things. Even the church Mary Langston attended began to refuse Black people! So she chose not to attend any church at all.

It must have made Langston's grandmother sad to see what had happened to her once-peaceful town. But Langston never saw her cry. And nobody ever cried in her stories. They fought, but they never cried.

Langston was thirteen when his grandmother died in 1915. And he didn't cry—though perhaps he wanted to. Once again, his life was uprooted.

His father still lived in Mexico. His mother worked in Illinois. Langston lived with friends of his grandmother's and remained in Kansas.

But Langston managed to find happiness. Thanks to his grandmother, Langston grew up to be a proud person, too. He was happy to be Black. And he felt ready to be brave.

CHAPTER 2
Class Poet

Langston's grandmother had taught him to be proud of being Black. When a famous Black scientist and teacher, Booker T. Washington, came to town, they had gone to hear him speak at the University of Kansas.

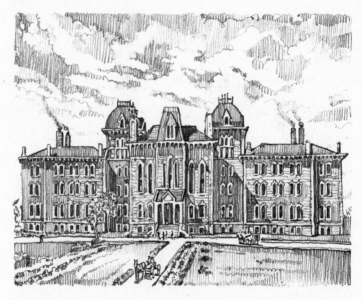

University of Kansas

Langston was given books to read by W. E. B. Du Bois, along with issues of the magazine the *Crisis*, which Du Bois edited. For entertainment,

Langston memorized poems by Paul Laurence Dunbar, an important Black poet. He realized the importance of education and studied hard to become a model student.

By 1916, Langston was yet again at a new school. When it came time to graduate eighth grade, he was elected class poet by his classmates. Langston had never written a poem in his life! But his teacher told him, "There's a first time for everything." Fourteen-year-old Langston decided to try! He wrote eight stanzas, one for each of his teachers—and eight more about his classmates. (A stanza is a group of lines separated from others in a poem.)

The day of the graduation ceremony, Langston was nervous. There was a chorus onstage, along with musicians and other performers. Langston sat separate from his class, facing the audience. His palms sweated as he waited for his turn to speak. When he stood, his knees shook. Langston's mouth went dry. But he read his poem, and everyone cheered. It was the first time Langston received applause in his entire life.

"It had never occurred to me to be a poet
before, or indeed a writer of any kind," Langston
remembered. His grandmother had given him a

deep love of stories and poetry, but always as a *reader*. Now Langston's dream was to be a *writer*!

Langston moved once again, this time to Cleveland, Ohio, with his mother and stepbrother. He read more than ever, and soon he had several favorite poets.

Edgar Lee Masters   Carl Sandburg

He admired the musical rhythms and rhymes of Vachel Lindsay and the storytelling in poems by Edgar Lee Masters. He admired Carl Sandburg, who wrote "free verse" (poems that didn't rhyme or have a regular rhythm).

Langston's favorite poet was Walt Whitman, who celebrated ordinary people and human experiences. Whitman's poems were free verse, too, but with surprising rhythms all their own. They reminded Langston of how people talked at church, repeating phrases to keep his attention.

Langston noticed the student magazine at his Ohio high school hadn't published writing by any of its Black students. He decided to submit his work. At first, his poems were rejected. But Langston didn't give up. Eventually, the magazine staff accepted a poem. Langston had been published!

Langston didn't notice at the time, but his earliest published poems used repetition much in the same way that Black religious folk songs, called spirituals, did. He had accidentally begun to invent his own style, which would come to incorporate other references to Black culture, including blues and work songs.

Walt Whitman (1819–1892)

Walt Whitman is one of America's most important poets. He was born in New York, half a century before the Civil War and the end of slavery. He wrote poems about democracy and freedom, often using the word "I" to represent people as a collective. His poems were often about individuality and human nature.

Whitman believed all people deserved freedom and dignity, and he used his writing to celebrate the American dream. His style was expansive, with long lines and musical-sounding repetition. His major collection of poems was *Leaves of Grass*. It was considered controversial at the time because it rejoiced in the human body. He revised it over and over again, producing nine editions of the book in his lifetime.

Just before Langston's senior year of high school, he received a letter from his father in Mexico. He invited Langston to come live with

him for the summer. Mr. Hughes was wealthy now and owned a ranch. Langston was eager to get to know the man, and to go on an adventure.

Sadly, the trip wasn't at all what Langston had expected. And neither was his father. In Mexico, people believed Langston's father was a dark-skinned white man, not Black at all. And Langston was forbidden from revealing the truth.

Even worse, he learned that his father *hated* Black people. He called them terrible names and believed untrue ideas about them. Langston's father offered to pay for Langston to go to college, but only if he studied to be a mine engineer and didn't become a writer. He wanted Langston to go to Switzerland after graduation, return to Mexico for work, and leave the United States for good. It would mean giving up everything Langston wanted for his own life.

Langston had one last year of high school to think about it. By the following summer, he would have to decide which direction his life would take.

CHAPTER 3
Far from Home

By the time Langston graduated high school, he had made his decision. He chose to follow his father to his ranch outside Mexico City. He packed what few belongings he could into an old suitcase and boarded a westbound train from

Ohio. His suitcase was filled with books and very heavy.

Langston didn't know when he might return home to his mother again. She was angry at him for choosing his father over her—and over his own dreams of becoming a writer. That morning, she left for work without even saying goodbye! Langston was sad as he watched the country pass by through the train window. The sun was low in the sky, and by the time the train approached the Mississippi River, sunset colors struck everything in Langston's view.

His mind wandered as he took in the orange and red light, which made the muddy water sparkle far below the bridge.

He thought about his father, and his terrible attitude toward Black people. He thought about his mother, still hard at work at a restaurant, who went to college but never achieved her dreams.

Langston pictured his beloved grandmother, recalling the stories she told about the Underground Railroad, freedom fighters, and fearless leaders. She had told him the frightening phrase "sold down the river," which meant being sold as property and sent down south to be auctioned off. Langston realized this was the exact river his grandmother had meant.

Langston had learned about Abraham Lincoln, how he had taken a raft all the way down the Mississippi to New Orleans. It was there Lincoln had witnessed slavery at its worst. Langston wondered if that was when Lincoln realized slavery was wrong.

Abraham Lincoln

The water swirled with color, and Langston's

mind raced. He thought of other rivers, in Africa and Asia, and how each of them had shaped the experiences of Black people in both good and bad ways.

Langston was inspired! His journal was stored away, so he pulled out the letter his father had written him and rushed to write on the back of the envelope.

The title came to him first: "The Negro Speaks of Rivers." And then the rest poured out of him as he tried to put his complicated feelings into poetry:

I've known rivers:
I've known rivers ancient as the world and older
than the flow of human blood in human veins.

My soul has grown deep like the rivers.

Langston was proud of the poem. When he got to Mexico, he told his father he didn't want to be an engineer after all. He wanted to be a writer! His father told Langston he wouldn't support such a foolish endeavor. And he certainly wouldn't pay for Langston to go to college in the United States.

Without telling his father, he typed out the poem and mailed it to an editor at the *Crisis*—the same magazine he remembered his grandmother sharing with him. Months later, he received word that they wanted to publish his poem!

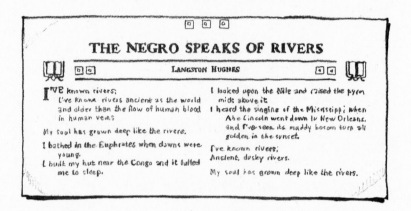

THE NEGRO SPEAKS OF RIVERS

LANGSTON HUGHES

I'VE known rivers:
   I've known rivers ancient as the world
   and older than the flow of human blood
   in human veins

My soul has grown deep like the rivers.

I bathed in the Euphrates when dawns were
   young.
I built my hut near the Congo and it lulled
   me to sleep.

I looked upon the Nile and raised the pyra-
   mids above it.
I heard the singing of the Mississippi when
   Abe Lincoln went down to New Orleans.
   and I've seen its muddy bosom turn all
   golden in the sunset.

I've known rivers:
Ancient, dusky rivers.

My soul has grown deep like the rivers.

When the issue came out, Langston showed his father. There his poem was, along with his name in print. But Langston's father didn't seem impressed. Instead, he asked how much the magazine had paid Langston for his work. Langston had to admit they hadn't paid him anything. Black publications didn't pay their contributors like white ones often did.

But Langston held true to his dreams. He

found work teaching English in Mexico. Eventually, his father gave in and agreed to pay for Langston to attend Columbia University in New York City.

CHAPTER 4
Reborn in Harlem

Langston Hughes arrived in New York at the perfect time. World War I was over, and the United States economy was booming. New York

City was now the world capital of manufacturing, culture, and business.

It was 1921. There were jobs to be had and opportunities for anyone willing to work hard. People flocked to the bustling city to start a new life, including thousands of Black people looking to escape the unfairness they faced in the segregated South.

Many of those Black people ended up in Harlem, a New York City neighborhood where African Americans outnumbered white people. Black artists and intellectuals from diverse backgrounds came together, exchanging ideas and celebrating new opportunities.

Fortunately for Langston, Harlem was a short walk from Columbia University's campus. His father had reserved a room for him at a dormitory there. Until his room was ready, he decided to stay at the YMCA on 135th Street. So many friendships were formed at that branch of the Y, it would later be referred to as "the living room of the Harlem Renaissance." Langston made the most of his three days there.

135th Street YMCA

The Harlem Renaissance

The word *renaissance* means "rebirth." During the 1920s, the New York neighborhood of Harlem experienced a dramatic revival—or rebirth. Black communities thrived there, leading to advancements in the creative arts, especially music and literature. The period is considered a golden age for Black culture in America.

Harlem became a destination for upwardly mobile Black people throughout the country, as well as white tourists eager to experience new forms of art and culture. Musicians like Duke Ellington and Louis Armstrong played exciting new music called "jazz." Singers Bessie Smith and Ethel Waters sang the "blues." Actors Florence Mills and Paul Robeson became popular on stage and screen. Visual artists like Aaron Douglas and Meta Vaux Warrick Fuller included African tribal imagery in their drawings and sculptures. Harlem became a great source of pride for Black people throughout the country and forever shaped the city of New York and the arts around the world.

Duke Ellington

When Langston went to campus to check into his dorm room, he was immediately reminded of the attitude against Black people outside of Harlem. The receptionist told Langston there weren't any rooms available. "They have all been reserved," she explained.

Langston told her he had a reservation. His father had made one from Mexico. But Langston's father had not identified Langston as Black. Roughly a dozen Black students had been accepted to Columbia that year, but they weren't allowed to live in the dormitories.

To make things worse, Langston was soon told his tuition hadn't been paid, though his father insisted the funds had been sent. Already, Langston did not feel very welcome at Columbia.

Langston was eventually given a room in Hartley Hall, Columbia's oldest dormitory. But he left campus every chance he got to return to his beloved Harlem. And he made friends at the public library there.

One close relationship was with Countee Cullen, another Black poet. He was one year younger than Langston, but the two had much in

Countee Cullen

common. Countee was well connected in the neighborhood, having moved to Harlem at the age of nine. His adopted father was a minister of the largest religious congregation in Harlem.

When Jessie Fauset, the *Crisis* editor who had published Langston's poem, learned that he was attending school in the city, she was quick to introduce him to well-known writers and thinkers. Through her, he met one of his idols, W. E. B. Du Bois. Through Countee, Langston met other publishers, including Alain Locke,

who would become an important promoter of Langston's poetry.

Langston spent the year attending lectures and readings at the library, and hearing jazz and blues performances at nightclubs. His studies suffered, as did his grades. But he was writing and publishing more than ever—and developing a style all his own! Langston wrote from the point of view of ordinary Black people in language that sounded the way people in Harlem actually talked. To him, it sounded like the spirit of jazz music itself.

In 1922, Langston dropped out of Columbia, in part so he could stop arguing with his father over finances. As much as he wanted a college education, he was learning much more from living and meeting people. For the first time in Langston's life, he didn't feel lonely. He felt like he finally fit in.

Langston decided to get a job. But he had a hard time finding one in Harlem. He found work in Staten Island that provided housing, but it was a very long train ride from the neighborhood where he felt he belonged.

The Jazz Age

Jazz was the music of the Harlem Renaissance.
It was the first American style of music to reach a
worldwide audience. In New York, people came
from all over the city to visit Harlem's nightclubs

and listen to jazz music. Jazz became so popular that the decade of the 1920s is also known as the Jazz Age.

Jazz is a uniquely African American combination of Black folk music and ragtime. The name *ragtime* refers to its faster pace and a melody that is syncopated, meaning the notes are out of their expected place in the beat.

Musicians from New Orleans, Louisiana, first played jazz in the late 1800s. Each musician brought their own culture to the collaboration of an individual song, from gospel to Spanish and African music. Rhythms sometimes changed within a song. Each musician was free to improvise, or make up their part, as they played. A jazz song could sound different every time it was heard!

If he couldn't live in Harlem, Langston thought he might as well leave the city. So he got a series of jobs on ships, and spent the next few years traveling the world, including in West Africa, France, and Italy.

Langston in Venice, Italy

Throughout his adventures, he kept in touch with the friends he had made, especially Countee Cullen. Langston would send him poems, and Countee would help get his work published.

In August 1923, the *Crisis* devoted an entire page to Langston's poems. And in 1924, Alain Locke began editing a special issue of the magazine *Survey Graphic*, called "Harlem: Mecca of the New Negro," which featured Langston prominently. Locke later expanded the issue into an anthology—a book that includes the writings of several authors.

By the time he returned to the United States in November 1924, Langston Hughes was a famous name in Harlem, and among many Black readers throughout the country. He was twenty-two years old and his star was on the rise!

CHAPTER 5
Always Moving On

Traveling outside the United States had changed Langston's perspective. Which is exactly what the young poet had wanted.

Du Bois had challenged Langston's generation to create their own Black culture. He called on them to create works so original and impactful, they might prove to white people how important Black culture was to the country. And perhaps finally, Black people would then be accepted as equal.

But how could Langston make something truly original, while honoring what had come before him?

When first sailing to Africa, Langston threw nearly every one of his books into the ocean off the coast of New Jersey. All except for one: a copy of Walt Whitman's *Leaves of Grass*. It was like tossing "a million bricks out of my heart," he later wrote.

He wanted to be free of everyone's expectations—those of his father and those of his mother. But also those of the writers and publishers in Harlem. He no longer felt as if he fit in with his intellectual friends, who seemed to care mostly about impressing one another. Instead, he wanted to write for everyday

working people. People who grew up poor, like he had.

Much of what Langston learned abroad surprised him. When his ship finally landed in Africa, he was disappointed when the locals he met didn't consider him a "Negro" at all. To them, he looked white!

"Unfortunately, I am not black," Langston wrote. "Here in the United States, the word 'Negro' is used to mean anyone who has any negro blood at all in his veins." But in Africa, Langston found that the word meant a person who was 100 percent Black, rather than light brown or olive yellow as his mother had been.

Like many Americans, Langston had a mixed heritage. Both of Langston's great-grandfathers on his father's side were white. One was a Jewish slave trader, the other Scottish. On his mother's side, he had French and Native American ancestry. Langston's own skin was a very light brown, and his black hair was straight.

It broke Langston's heart not to be accepted as Black by people in Africa. It seemed like he might not be truly accepted anywhere.

When Langston returned to the United States, he still didn't have a way to support himself. Langston's dreams of college had returned.

This time, he wanted to go to a Black college—
one that would teach him about the history and
legacy of his people. Unfortunately, that meant
leaving New York.

Langston traveled to Washington, DC, where
his mother and stepbrother were living with
wealthy relatives. They invited Langston to live
with them as well. Langston found his relatives
snobbish. They didn't respect Black people any

more than his father had. They teased him for wanting a working-class job, and not a more intellectual one. Worse, they didn't approve of his poems!

They didn't understand why Langston used language that sounded the way people actually spoke. To them, respectable poetry used proper English and was limited to polite topics. When the *Crisis* published Langston's poem "Song to a Negro Wash-Woman," his relatives criticized him. Langston, his mother, and his stepbrother moved into a two-room apartment of their own. It had no heat, but they made do.

Langston made a small amount of money publishing articles and stories. He made new connections, as well, including Georgia Douglas

Georgia Douglas Johnson

Johnson, who organized readings and events. She urged Langston to submit a long, moody poem to a contest. Langston won! And his poem was read aloud by James Weldon Johnson, another of Langston's heroes.

At the ceremony, he met Zora Neale Hurston, a fellow prize winner. He also met Carl Van Vechten, a writer for the magazine *Vanity Fair*, which had a large white audience. Van Vechten published some of Langston's poems. It was the first time he was paid for his poetry. Through Van Vechten's connections, Langston was also offered a book deal with Alfred A. Knopf. It seemed to Langston that making a living as a poet wasn't such a far-fetched dream after all.

Carl Van Vechten

While working at the Wardman Park Hotel, Langston was "discovered" by Vachel Lindsay, the most popular poet touring in America. Lindsay was known for giving sold-out readings of poems—many of which were written to be sung or chanted.

Although Langston was already famous in certain circles, his audience was mostly Black. Langston loved that fact, but to earn a living, he needed a larger audience. And that's precisely what Lindsay's publicity offered him.

Zora Neale Hurston (1891–1960)

Born in Alabama and raised in Florida, Zora Neale Hurston had a lifelong interest in the rural folktales of the American South. She moved to Harlem in 1925, and in 1927 began collecting and publishing folktales, songs, sermons, and jokes, both in the United States and the Caribbean. Alongside Langston Hughes, she was a leading voice of the Harlem Renaissance.

Zora loved anthropology, the study of people and their cultures, more than literature. She incorporated what she learned into her own plays and stories. Her best-known work is the novel *Their Eyes Were Watching God*, which was published in 1937. It used humor to examine how society treated Black women.

Following the articles about Langston Hughes, the "busboy poet," in 1925, Lindsay incorporated Langston's poems into his performances twice more, further broadening his audience. And what great timing! When Langston's first book of poems, *The Weary Blues*, was published the following year, it was a success—with Black *and* white readers.

Finally, Langston could afford to attend college. He enrolled at a prestigious all-Black school, Lincoln University, in Pennsylvania. Once again, he was on the move.

CHAPTER 6
Poet on Tour

Lincoln University

Langston's college years were possibly his happiest. "My years there were happy years, jolly and full of fun," he wrote. Three hundred students (all of them male) were enrolled at the university, and Langston, now twenty-four, quickly made friends. He attended classes during the week. On weekends, he toured and read from *The Weary Blues.*

Having a published book made Langston somewhat of a celebrity on campus. The school's vocal quartet often accompanied him on the road, performing at Black churches and schools. Langston sold copies of his book, and people waited in line for his autograph.

Langston read in Cleveland, Ohio, where he had graduated from high school. But Langston hadn't lived in the city very long, and he was nervous. As he stepped to the podium, Langston recognized several teachers and classmates, all smiling at him with pride. They, too, wanted him to sign copies of his book for them.

And Langston read at Oberlin College, where his beloved grandmother had studied. Langston wanted to cry as he told the audience about his grandmother's life, and the stories she would tell. But he remembered her advice to him as a boy sitting on her knee: "Crying doesn't help a thing."

One day, Langston received a large envelope from a magazine called the *Nation*. The editor had enclosed a copy of an essay that was to appear in the magazine. It was by a Black newspaper editor named George Schuyler, who said that he didn't believe in "American Negro art" at all! He argued that the best work by Black people was no different than that of white

George Schuyler

people. He considered jazz, blues, and other art forms coming out of Harlem to be "folk art," and nothing new. By calling it folk art, he meant that it was more simplistic or common, unlike fine art, which is produced by people who study for years in order to create it.

Langston was invited to respond to Schuyler's essay. He replied with his own, and it was unlike anything he had written before. His poems were always in other people's voices, not his own.

This was a chance to tell the world what he, himself, really thought.

Langston's essay "The Negro Artist and the Racial Mountain" explained his philosophy. Trying to fit into a white standard, Langston argued, was the greatest obstacle of any Black artist, and true art *shouldn't* fit in. He insisted that ordinary people were worth celebrating, even if they were "low-down folks." Langston knew he wasn't the only artist in Harlem who felt this way. "We . . . intend to express our individual dark-skinned selves without fear or shame," he wrote. "If white people are pleased we are glad. If they are not, it doesn't matter. We know we are beautiful. And ugly too."

The *Nation* published Schuyler's article in June 1926. They published Langston's response one week later. The ideas in Langston's essay spread through Harlem like wildfire! It became a rallying cry for Black artists all over the country.

The Negro Artist and the Racial Mountian

Langston By Langston Hughes Hughes

written at Ranch Honnariett
Spring 1926

Langston's words had given Black artists permission to be more true to themselves and their heritage.

The Weary Blues quickly sold out. By Langston's first summer at Lincoln, he had earned out his advance—the money he was paid to write the book in advance of its publication. From that day on, with every copy Langston's publisher sold, he would receive some of the profits. Langston often spent the money he made from book sales on travel expenses for his tour. He loved meeting new people everywhere he went.

When Langston wasn't in class or giving readings, he was back in Harlem. It felt like his true home. Each time he returned, he was treated like family. Everyone seemed to want to meet him. Editors wanted his poems. Younger writers wanted his advice. Some writers even wanted to team up with Langston to create new work.

Zora Neale Hurston was one of those writers. They collaborated on stories and plays. Together with other friends, Zora and Langston started their own literary magazine, which they called *Fire!!* Langston wrote that they wanted to "burn up a lot of the old, dead conventional Negro-white ideas of the past."

Alongside their own writing, they published important Black authors of their day, including Arna Bontemps, Helene Johnson, and Langston's friend Countee Cullen.

Langston started writing short stories as well. Soon, he was publishing them as often as his poems. George Schuyler, the editor who had called Langston's writing "folk art," even published three of Langston's stories in his magazine, the *Messenger*.

Wealthy patrons took notice of Langston. Suddenly, people were willing to pay his living and travel expenses. Langston was able to take his tour farther. During his final two years of college, Langston gave readings throughout the South. In July 1927, he and Zora toured the South together, meeting people and writing down folk songs and stories. Langston's poems reflected the voices of the people he met.

While still studying at Lincoln, Langston published a second book of poems and wrote a novel. His poems were chosen for a collection called *Modern American and British Poetry*. It featured the most influential poets of the time, regardless of their race.

When Langston graduated from college in the spring of 1929, he felt unstoppable. He didn't know that by the end of the year, the whole world would have changed.

The Great Depression in Harlem

On October 29, 1929, the stock market crashed. The effects were immediate and worldwide. Thousands of people lost their life savings and many workers lost their jobs. This is known as the Great Depression.

In Harlem, the unemployment rate approached 50 percent. Almost half of the households in Harlem took in lodgers for extra income. By 1933, the neighborhood had the worst living conditions in the city.

Residents stuck together, for the most part. Families swapped or borrowed goods to save money. They loaned one another money when they could. Focused on survival, people didn't have time for music and poetry. Tourists from other parts of the city stopped coming. By the mid-1930s, the Harlem Renaissance was over.

CHAPTER 7
Finding Community Abroad

"The depression brought everybody down a peg or two," wrote Langston. "And the Negroes had but few pegs to fall." This meant that they were already quite near the bottom economically.

Black artists left the city rather than go hungry. Magazines stopped giving cash prizes. Friends and collaborators suddenly had to compete for whatever few resources remained. Langston no longer had the support of patrons. All he had was his dream, and the will to make it come true.

In 1930, Langston's novel *Not Without Laughter* was published. He won a prestigious prize, the Harmon Gold Medal for literature. It came with a $400 cash prize. It was enough money for Langston to leave New York.

Langston printed cheap editions of his poems and toured the South, selling them to readers unable to afford his books. Around that time, nine Black teenagers nicknamed the Scottsboro Boys were arrested in Alabama for crimes they didn't commit. When the trial took place in 1932, Langston followed it closely in the news. He published *Scottsboro Limited: Four Poems and a Play* later that year.

The Scottsboro Boys

Langston wrote a children's book with fellow Harlem Renaissance poet Arna Bontemps. *Popo and Fifina* was about the everyday life of a Black working-class Haitian family. Haiti was the first Black republic, and Langston had traveled there to see what it was like. The story was relatable to children growing up in the United States during the Great Depression. Langston also wrote a collection of poems for children called *The Dream Keeper and Other Poems*. It contains the famous poem "Let America Be America Again."

Back in Harlem, conditions had worsened. Hundreds of people were being evicted from their homes each week. The government was doing little to help. People turned to one another, but it was a struggle just to help themselves.

A new political group called the Communist Party believed the government should protect the working class. In Harlem, they fought to keep people in their homes. In the South, they organized and paid for the Scottsboro Boys' legal defense. Black Americans took notice. Many were moved to see white people take to the streets to protest the injustice.

Communism was a new idea in the world. In 1917, toward the end of World War I, a revolution in Russia had overthrown their monarchy and replaced it with a different form of government. They founded a new country called the Soviet Union. Communists believed property ownership and profitmaking had led to inequality and suffering, and that the people should collectively own all land and industry. Their ideas had spread to the United States and around the world.

A decade earlier, the Communists were seen as out of touch with the times. Suddenly, their ideas were catching on, especially among poor Americans who had fallen on hard times.

Langston joined a group of Black artists on their way to the Soviet Union. His writing called for reform and became more extreme. Langston sent poems and stories back to the United States for publication. He spent a year in Moscow, the capital of the Soviet Union, then toured Asia—visiting Japan, Korea, and China—before ending his travels in Hawaii.

When he reached Hawaii, an FBI agent was waiting for him. They didn't arrest him. He hadn't committed any crimes. But they listened carefully to what Langston told the press. Though Langston wasn't an official member of the Communist Party, he was unapologetic in his support of their cause. In the coming years, Langston's beliefs and writings would cause him trouble.

Langston in Moscow

CHAPTER 8
Political Poet

Langston continued to write and publish, including a short story collection and several plays. In 1940, when he was thirty-eight, he published a book about his life, *The Big Sea*. Today, it is considered the finest firsthand account of the Harlem Renaissance. At the time it was published, however, it did not sell well. Communism and Communists were seen as negative influences in the United States. The political views Langston expressed in his twenties led to controversy in his forties. Many of his lectures and readings were canceled due to protests.

A younger Black writer, Richard Wright, published his novel *Native Son* the same year. It sold very well and won the Spingarn Medal, a prize Langston had hoped his own book would win. Langston was no longer the most famous Black writer in America. He feared his best days were behind him.

Langston again struggled to earn a living. In 1941, the Japanese attack on Pearl Harbor, Hawaii, pulled the United States into World War II. The nation's attention turned to the war effort.

Langston was too old to be drafted for military service. So beginning in November of 1942, he wrote a weekly newspaper column in the *Chicago Defender* to speak out against America's enemies in the war. Langston invented a character named Jesse B. Semple, a cartoonish "simple minded friend" whose made-up conversations explored

real-world issues. Readers of the paper embraced his articles, and Langston continued to write them for twenty years.

In 1945, World War II ended. The Soviet Union, which had been an ally of the United States during the war, quickly became an enemy. Communists in the Soviet Union had taken away citizens' rights and freedoms. Americans feared the Communist Party at home. Congress formed a committee to investigate Communist activity within the United States.

In 1951, a group of former FBI agents published a report about Communist influence that named people suspected of being dangerous to American democracy. Like many other outspoken Black activists, Langston was among those listed.

People continued to protest Langston whenever

he appeared in public—except for in the South. There, Black audiences were less interested in his politics than in his message of empowerment.

The ongoing debate didn't stop Langston from publishing. That same year, he published *Montage of a Dream Deferred*. (*Deferred* means to be delayed.) The book contains some of the most famous lines in all of American poetry and is widely quoted still today. The opening lines to Langston's poem "Harlem" asks:

What happens to a dream deferred?
Does it dry up
like a raisin in the sun?

In 1953, Langston was ordered to appear before the US Senate. Langston had an impossible decision to make. He could refuse to appear and risk being jailed. He could invoke the Fifth Amendment of the US Constitution, which gave Langston the right not to answer questions that would make him appear guilty. Or he could cooperate as a "friendly witness." By doing so, Langston knew he would be asked under oath to identify his friends and colleagues.

On March 24, 1953, Langston was questioned in private. He believed that by doing so, he could clear his name and save his reputation. Langston pushed back on the committee's questions. He corrected misstatements and said he had broken no laws. He stood up for his beliefs and spoke out strongly against segregation, putting on the record many of the injustices he personally faced in his life.

"I do not believe that the desire for change, and working toward it, is necessarily un-American," Langston argued.

Langston's interviewers quoted his most political poetry back to him and tried to make him feel ashamed for the views he held in his youth. Langston said that his views had changed. On the question of his guilt or innocence,

Langston did not budge. Langston stressed that he believed in the democratic process, and that he never wished for the United States to change its form of government. He insisted that the

changes he wrote about should be made through voting.

At one point, Langston read the lyrics of "I Dream a World," a song he had written for the opera *Troubled Island*:

A world I dream where black or white,
Whatever race you be,
Will share the bounties of the earth
And every man is free.

When it came time to give his public testimony, Langston defended his writing and his belief in the American dream. And he did so without "naming names" of Communists, as the committee had wanted.

Langston did, however, claim that enough progress had been made in America that he no longer believed in certain Communist principles. That disappointed a lot of Black artists. They no longer saw Langston as a leader in the fight for justice.

CHAPTER 9
The Dream Keeper

Toward the end of his life, Langston continued to publish poetry, plays, lyrics, articles, and other types of writing. Inspired by the stories he first learned from his grandmother, Langston wrote profiles of Americans who made important contributions to American Black identity. He edited influential anthologies of Black poetry.

Langston chronicled the history of the NAACP (the National Association for the Advancement of Colored People), a leading civil rights organization. It is the NAACP that awards the Spingarn Medal annually. Writing about the people and goals of the organization, mixed with his own memories and stories,

Langston produced *Fight for Freedom*. It was a widely celebrated account of the civil rights movement from 1909 to 1962.

When he wasn't writing, Langston continued to mentor and promote younger writers. He corresponded with poets from around the world, offering encouragement and advice. He even lived to see someone he had mentored, Gwendolyn Brooks, win the Pulitzer Prize for Poetry! She was the first Black person to do so.

Langston and Gwendolyn Brooks

Toward the end of his life, Langston witnessed a return to popularity. In 1958, *LIFE* magazine ran a feature story celebrating him as someone "who brought honor to the United States." It was hard to imagine that less than ten years before, the same magazine had warned its readers about Langston, labeling him as a dangerous Communist.

Langston received an honorary doctorate

degree from Howard University, a school he couldn't afford to attend when he was younger. And he was invited to the White House—twice!

In 1960, Langston won the Spingarn Medal. It was the prize he had been hoping to win for twenty years. In his acceptance speech, Langston urged young Black writers to write honestly about their lives, and about their dreams. And in 1962, when he was sixty years old, Langston served on a panel during the first national poetry festival. He received a standing ovation.

The Spingarn Medal

Awarded annually since 1915, the Spingarn Medal honors African Americans who have "made the highest achievement" in "any honorable field." The NAACP administers the award, and has bestowed it to writers, artists, athletes, entertainers, politicians, and other cultural figures. Past recipients of the prize include W. E. B. Du Bois (1920), Martin Luther King Jr. (1957), Duke Ellington (1959), Hank Aaron (1975), Rosa Parks (1979), Lena Horne (1983), Maya Angelou (1994), Oprah Winfrey (2000), John Lewis (2002), Quincy Jones (2014), and Sidney Poitier (2015).

Langston Hughes died on May 22, 1967, due to an infection following surgery for cancer. As per Langston's instructions, no words were read at his memorial service. A pianist played jazz and blues at his funeral, along with a drummer and bass player. Those in attendance both laughed and cried, just as Langston would have wanted.

On December 24, 1967, Martin Luther King Jr. invoked Langston's legacy when giving a sermon at the Ebenezer Baptist Church in Atlanta, Georgia. In the widely broadcast speech, King admits: "I am personally the victim of deferred dreams." He was referencing the famous lines from Langston's poem "Harlem."

Twenty years after his death, Langston's ashes were laid to rest under the floor of the lobby of the New York Public Library's Schomburg Center for Research in Black Culture in Harlem. Famous Black poets, including Maya Angelou and Amiri Baraka, were at the ceremony.

In 2001, the Academy of American Poets celebrated National Poetry Month by asking visitors to its popular website to vote for a poet to appear on a postage stamp. Langston, who remains among the site's most popular poets (along with Robert Frost, Emily Dickinson, and Walt Whitman), was chosen by a wide margin.

The US Postal Service issued a Langston Hughes stamp in January 2002. Today, Langston Hughes's dreams—and his words—live on in the imaginations of people throughout the world.

Timeline of Langston Hughes's Life

1902	James Langston Hughes is born in Joplin, Missouri
1907	Visits Mexico City with his mother and father
1915	His grandmother, Mary Langston, dies in Lawrence, Kansas
1920	Graduates from Central High School in Cleveland, Ohio
	Lives with his father outside of Mexico City
1921	Publishes "The Negro Speaks of Rivers" in the *Crisis* magazine
	First visits Harlem while enrolled at Columbia University
1923	Sails to West Africa
1925	Promoted by Vachel Lindsay as a "busboy poet"
1926	Enrolls at Lincoln University
	Publishes first book of poems, *The Weary Blues*
	Writes "The Negro Artist and the Racial Mountain"
1932	Publishes *The Dream Keeper* and two other books
1933	Lives in Moscow and tours Asia
1940	Publishes autobiography, *The Big Sea*
1951	Publishes *Montage of a Dream Deferred*
1960	Wins NAACP's Spingarn Medal
1967	Dies on May 22 in New York City

Timeline of the World

1902 — Theodore Roosevelt becomes first US president to ride in an automobile

1903 — W. E. B. Du Bois publishes *The Souls of Black Folk*

1909 — NAACP is founded in New York City

1914 — World War I begins in Europe

— Panama Canal opens

1920 — Women are granted the right to vote in the United States

1928 — Mickey Mouse appears in *Steamboat Willie*, the first cartoon with sound

1929 — The Great Depression begins, the worst economic decline in world history

1940 — Hattie McDaniel becomes first Black actor to win an Academy Award for the role of Mammy in *Gone with the Wind*

1945 — World War II ends

1947 — Jackie Robinson of the Brooklyn Dodgers becomes first Black person to play major league baseball

1963 — Martin Luther King Jr. delivers famous "I Have a Dream" speech during the March on Washington for Jobs and Freedom

1965 — Voting Rights Act passes, making racial discrimination in voting illegal

Bibliography

Berry, Faith. *Langston Hughes: Before and Beyond Harlem*. Westport, Connecticut: Lawrence Hill & Company, 1983.

Hughes, Langston. *The Big Sea*. New York: Knopf, 1940.

Hughes, Langston. *I Wonder As I Wander*. New York: Rinehart, 1956.

Leach, Laurie F. *Langston Hughes: A Biography*. Westport, Connecticut: Greenwood Press, 2004.

Low, Denise, and T.F. Pecore Weso. *Langston Hughes in Lawrence: Photographs & Biographical Resources*. Lawrence, Kansas: Mammoth Publications, 2004.